EMMANUEL JOSEPH

The Quest for Knowledge, Bridging Education, Gaming, and Spiritual Growth

Copyright © 2025 by Emmanuel Joseph

All rights reserved. No part of this publication may be reproduced, stored or transmitted in any form or by any means, electronic, mechanical, photocopying, recording, scanning, or otherwise without written permission from the publisher. It is illegal to copy this book, post it to a website, or distribute it by any other means without permission.

First edition

This book was professionally typeset on Reedsy. Find out more at reedsy.com

Contents

1	Chapter 1: The Pursuit of Knowledge	1
2	Chapter 2: The Role of Formal Education	3
3	Chapter 3: The Evolution of Gaming	5
4	Chapter 4: The Intersection of Education and Gaming	7
5	Chapter 5: Gamification and Motivation	9
6	Chapter 6: Spiritual Growth and Self-Discovery	11
7	Chapter 7: Integrating Knowledge and Wisdom	13
8	Chapter 8: Bridging the Gap Between Education and...	15
9	Chapter 9: The Power of Mindfulness in Learning	17
10	Chapter 10: The Impact of Technology on Learning	19
11	Chapter 11: Embracing Lifelong Learning	21
12	Chapter 12: The Future of Knowledge and Growth	23
13	Chapter 13: The Synergy of Creativity and Knowledge	25
14	Chapter 14: Cultivating a Growth Mindset	27
15	Chapter 15: The Role of Mentorship and Community	29

1

Chapter 1: The Pursuit of Knowledge

In the pursuit of knowledge, we often find ourselves at the intersection of education, personal interests, and spiritual growth. This quest is more than a journey through the traditional halls of learning; it's an expedition that touches every aspect of our lives. The drive to understand the world around us and our place within it is intrinsic to human nature. As we embark on this quest, we discover that knowledge comes in various forms and from countless sources. Whether it's through formal education, life experiences, or spiritual introspection, each path offers unique insights that contribute to our overall understanding.

Education has always been the cornerstone of knowledge acquisition. Through structured learning, we gain access to a wealth of information that builds the foundation for our intellectual growth. Schools, colleges, and universities provide a systematic approach to learning, ensuring that we grasp the essential concepts and skills needed to navigate the complexities of the modern world. However, the limitations of formal education become evident when we consider the vast expanse of human knowledge that lies beyond the classroom. To truly embrace our quest for knowledge, we must look beyond traditional education and explore alternative avenues.

One such avenue is the world of gaming. Often dismissed as mere entertainment, games have evolved into powerful tools for learning and personal development. Educational games, in particular, have the potential to engage students in ways that traditional methods cannot. By presenting information in an interactive and immersive format, games can make learning more enjoyable and memorable. Moreover, gaming fosters critical thinking, problem-solving, and collaboration skills, which are essential for success in both academic and professional settings. As we delve deeper into the role of gaming in education, we begin to appreciate its potential to bridge the gap between knowledge and application.

Spiritual growth, on the other hand, offers a different dimension to our quest for knowledge. While education and gaming primarily focus on external understanding, spirituality encourages us to look inward and explore our inner selves. Through practices such as meditation, mindfulness, and prayer, we develop a deeper connection with our true nature and the universe. This inner journey helps us cultivate wisdom, compassion, and resilience, which are invaluable qualities for navigating the challenges of life. As we integrate spiritual growth into our pursuit of knowledge, we create a holistic approach that nurtures both our intellect and our soul.

2

Chapter 2: The Role of Formal Education

Formal education has long been regarded as the primary means of acquiring knowledge. From early childhood through adulthood, we are taught to value structured learning environments that provide a systematic approach to education. Schools, colleges, and universities offer a curriculum designed to impart essential knowledge and skills, preparing students for their future careers and personal lives. This traditional model of education has proven effective in many ways, but it also has its limitations. As we seek to expand our understanding, we must recognize the need to complement formal education with other forms of learning.

One of the strengths of formal education is its ability to provide a comprehensive foundation in various subjects. Through a well-rounded curriculum, students gain exposure to a wide range of disciplines, from mathematics and science to literature and history. This broad base of knowledge equips individuals with the critical thinking and problem-solving skills necessary to succeed in a rapidly changing world. Moreover, formal education fosters a sense of discipline and perseverance, as students learn to navigate the demands of academic life. However, the structured nature of formal education can sometimes stifle creativity and limit the exploration of individual interests.

To address these limitations, educators and policymakers must consider ways to incorporate more flexible and personalized approaches to learning.

By allowing students to pursue their passions and interests, we can create a more engaging and meaningful educational experience. This could involve offering a variety of elective courses, encouraging independent projects, and providing opportunities for experiential learning. By embracing a more holistic approach to education, we can better prepare students for the complexities of the modern world and empower them to become lifelong learners.

Another important aspect of formal education is the role of teachers and mentors. Educators play a crucial role in shaping the minds and hearts of their students, guiding them on their journey of discovery. Through their expertise, passion, and dedication, teachers inspire students to reach their full potential and develop a love for learning. In addition to imparting knowledge, educators also serve as role models, demonstrating the values of curiosity, integrity, and perseverance. As we continue to evolve our educational systems, we must ensure that teachers receive the support and resources they need to thrive in their roles.

Finally, we must recognize the importance of creating inclusive and equitable educational environments. Access to quality education is a fundamental human right, and it is essential that all individuals, regardless of their background or circumstances, have the opportunity to pursue their quest for knowledge. By addressing disparities in education and fostering a culture of inclusivity, we can create a more just and enlightened society. As we strive to bridge the gap between education, gaming, and spiritual growth, we must remain committed to the principles of equity and inclusion.

3

Chapter 3: The Evolution of Gaming

Gaming has undergone a remarkable transformation over the past few decades. What was once considered a niche hobby has evolved into a global phenomenon that transcends age, culture, and geography. From simple 8-bit graphics to immersive virtual reality experiences, the world of gaming has expanded in ways that few could have imagined. As technology continues to advance, games have become more sophisticated, offering players new and exciting ways to engage with digital content. In this chapter, we explore the evolution of gaming and its potential to serve as a powerful tool for education and personal development.

The early days of gaming were characterized by simple yet addictive gameplay. Classics like Pac-Man, Space Invaders, and Super Mario Bros. captured the imagination of players around the world, laying the foundation for the gaming industry as we know it today. These early games were designed primarily for entertainment, offering players a fun and engaging way to pass the time. However, as technology progressed, developers began to experiment with more complex game mechanics and narratives, paving the way for a new era of gaming.

One of the most significant developments in the evolution of gaming is the rise of educational games. Recognizing the potential of games to engage and educate, developers have created a wide range of titles designed to teach various subjects and skills. From math and science to language and history, educational games offer a unique and interactive way to learn. By combining the elements of play and learning, these games can make education more enjoyable and effective. Moreover, educational games can cater to different learning styles, allowing students to grasp concepts at their own pace and in their own way.

In addition to educational games, the gaming industry has also seen the rise of serious games, which are designed to address real-world issues and promote social change. These games tackle topics such as environmental conservation, mental health, and conflict resolution, encouraging players to think critically and empathetically about the world around them. By immersing players in meaningful narratives and challenging them to make decisions with real-world implications, serious games can foster a deeper understanding of complex issues and inspire positive action.

As we look to the future of gaming, we can expect continued advancements in technology and game design. Virtual reality, augmented reality, and artificial intelligence are just a few of the innovations that have the potential to revolutionize the gaming experience. These technologies can create even more immersive and interactive environments, offering players new ways to explore, learn, and grow. As we embrace the potential of gaming, we must also consider the ethical implications and strive to create games that are inclusive, responsible, and beneficial to society.

4

Chapter 4: The Intersection of Education and Gaming

The intersection of education and gaming is a fascinating and rapidly evolving field. As we explore the potential of games to enhance learning, we begin to see the possibilities for a more engaging and effective educational experience. By harnessing the power of interactive and immersive gameplay, educators can create dynamic learning environments that cater to diverse learning styles and foster a love for learning. In this chapter, we delve into the ways in which gaming and education can complement and enrich each other.

One of the key benefits of integrating gaming into education is the ability to make learning more enjoyable and engaging. Traditional teaching methods can sometimes feel monotonous and disconnected from real-life applications. In contrast, games provide an interactive and hands-on approach to learning, allowing students to actively participate in their education. By presenting information in a game-like format, educators can capture students' attention and motivate them to explore new concepts and ideas. This increased engagement can lead to better retention and comprehension of the material.

Another advantage of educational gaming is the ability to cater to different learning styles and paces. Every student learns differently, and traditional education often struggles to accommodate these differences. Games, however, can be designed to offer multiple pathways to understanding, allowing students to learn in the way that suits them best. Whether through visual, auditory, or kinesthetic means, educational games can provide a personalized learning experience that meets the needs of each individual. Additionally, games can offer immediate feedback and reinforcement, helping students to identify and correct mistakes in real-time.

Collaboration and teamwork are also important aspects of educational gaming. Many games require players to work together to achieve common goals, fostering a sense of community and cooperation. In a classroom setting, this can translate to group projects and collaborative learning activities that encourage students to share ideas and support each other. By promoting teamwork and communication skills, educational games can help students develop the social and interpersonal skills needed for success in both academic and professional settings.

Finally, the use of gaming in education can help bridge the gap between theory and practice. Many traditional educational methods focus on abstract concepts and theoretical knowledge, which can be difficult for students to apply in real-world situations. Games, on the other hand, offer a practical and experiential approach to learning. By simulating real-world scenarios and challenges, games allow students to apply their knowledge and skills in a meaningful context. This hands-on experience can help students develop a deeper understanding of the material and better prepare them for future understanding and skill development.

5

Chapter 5: Gamification and Motivation

Gamification, the application of game elements to non-game contexts, has gained significant traction in recent years. By incorporating elements such as points, badges, and leaderboards, educators and organizations can tap into the motivational power of games to enhance engagement and performance. In this chapter, we explore the principles of gamification and its potential to transform the way we learn and achieve our goals.

One of the key principles of gamification is the concept of rewards and recognition. In games, players are often motivated by the prospect of earning points, leveling up, and unlocking achievements. These rewards provide a sense of accomplishment and progress, encouraging players to continue their efforts. By integrating similar elements into educational and professional settings, we can create a more motivating and rewarding experience. For example, students can earn badges for completing assignments, participate in competitive quizzes, or track their progress through a points system. This approach can make learning more enjoyable and encourage a sense of achievement.

Another important aspect of gamification is the use of challenges and quests. Games often present players with a series of challenges that require them to solve problems, make decisions, and overcome obstacles. These challenges provide a sense of purpose and direction, driving players to engage more deeply with the game. By incorporating challenges and quests into educational activities, we can create a more immersive and engaging learning experience. For instance, students can embark on virtual quests that require them to apply their knowledge and skills to solve real-world problems. This approach not only enhances motivation but also fosters critical thinking and problem-solving abilities.

Feedback and progression are also crucial elements of gamification. In games, players receive immediate feedback on their actions, allowing them to learn from their mistakes and make improvements. This continuous feedback loop is essential for skill development and mastery. By providing timely and constructive feedback in educational settings, we can help students understand their strengths and areas for improvement. Additionally, games often feature progression systems that allow players to track their growth and development. Implementing similar systems in education can help students visualize their progress and stay motivated to achieve their goals.

Finally, gamification can foster a sense of community and collaboration. Many games encourage players to work together, share resources, and support each other's efforts. By creating opportunities for collaboration in educational settings, we can promote teamwork and social interaction. For example, students can participate in group projects, collaborate on problem-solving tasks, and share their achievements with their peers. This sense of community can enhance motivation and create a supportive learning environment.

6

Chapter 6: Spiritual Growth and Self-Discovery

While education and gaming primarily focus on external knowledge and skills, spiritual growth invites us to turn inward and explore our inner selves. This journey of self-discovery helps us develop a deeper understanding of our true nature, values, and purpose. In this chapter, we delve into the importance of spiritual growth and its role in our quest for knowledge.

Spiritual growth begins with self-awareness. By taking the time to reflect on our thoughts, emotions, and experiences, we can gain insights into our true selves. Practices such as meditation, mindfulness, and journaling can help us cultivate self-awareness and develop a greater sense of clarity and peace. As we become more attuned to our inner world, we can identify our strengths, weaknesses, and aspirations, guiding us on our path of growth and self-improvement.

Another important aspect of spiritual growth is the development of compassion and empathy. By connecting with our inner selves, we can cultivate a greater sense of understanding and kindness toward others. Practices such as loving-kindness meditation and acts of service can help us develop these qualities, fostering a sense of interconnectedness and harmony. As we nurture our compassion and empathy, we become more attuned to the needs and experiences of those around us, enhancing our relationships and contributing to a more compassionate world.

Spiritual growth also involves exploring our values and purpose. By reflecting on what truly matters to us, we can align our actions and decisions with our core beliefs. This sense of purpose provides direction and meaning to our lives, motivating us to pursue our goals with passion and dedication. Whether through career, hobbies, or community involvement, living in alignment with our values can lead to a more fulfilling and meaningful life.

Finally, spiritual growth encourages us to embrace the unknown and cultivate a sense of wonder and curiosity. Life is full of mysteries and uncertainties, and by approaching these with an open mind and heart, we can continue to learn and grow. Practices such as contemplative prayer, nature walks, and creative expression can help us connect with the beauty and wonder of the world, inspiring us to explore new horizons and expand our understanding.

7

Chapter 7: Integrating Knowledge and Wisdom

As we journey through our quest for knowledge, it is essential to integrate the various forms of understanding we acquire. By combining intellectual knowledge, practical skills, and spiritual wisdom, we can create a holistic approach to learning and growth. In this chapter, we explore the importance of integrating knowledge and wisdom and how it can enhance our lives.

Intellectual knowledge provides us with the information and concepts needed to understand the world around us. Through formal education and self-directed learning, we gain access to a wealth of knowledge that forms the foundation of our understanding. However, intellectual knowledge alone is not sufficient for navigating the complexities of life. We must also develop practical skills that allow us to apply our knowledge in real-world situations.

Practical skills are the abilities and competencies needed to perform tasks and solve problems. These skills can be acquired through hands-on experiences, practice, and experimentation. By developing practical skills, we can translate our intellectual knowledge into tangible outcomes and achievements. For example, understanding the principles of mathematics is important, but the ability to apply these principles to solve real-world problems is what makes the knowledge truly valuable.

Spiritual wisdom, on the other hand, offers a deeper and more intuitive understanding of ourselves and the world. This wisdom is cultivated through practices such as meditation, reflection, and contemplation. By connecting with our inner selves and the greater universe, we can gain insights that go beyond intellectual knowledge. Spiritual wisdom helps us develop qualities such as compassion, resilience, and clarity, which are essential for navigating the challenges and uncertainties of life.

To integrate knowledge and wisdom, we must adopt a holistic approach to learning and growth. This involves recognizing the interconnectedness of different forms of understanding and seeking to balance them in our lives. For example, we can combine intellectual study with hands-on practice and spiritual reflection to create a more comprehensive and meaningful learning experience. By integrating these elements, we can develop a well-rounded and adaptable approach to life, capable of meeting the demands of an ever-changing world.

Another important aspect of integrating knowledge and wisdom is the recognition of lifelong learning. Our quest for knowledge does not end with formal education or the acquisition of specific skills. It is an ongoing journey that requires us to remain curious, open-minded, and receptive to new experiences. By embracing the concept of lifelong learning, we can continue to grow and evolve, enriching our lives and contributing to the betterment of society.

8

Chapter 8: Bridging the Gap Between Education and Spirituality

The relationship between education and spirituality is often viewed as distinct and separate. However, there is a growing recognition of the need to bridge the gap between these two realms, creating a more integrated and holistic approach to learning and growth. In this chapter, we explore the ways in which education and spirituality can complement and enhance each other.

One of the key areas of intersection between education and spirituality is the development of self-awareness and emotional intelligence. Traditional education often focuses on cognitive and intellectual development, but it is equally important to nurture our emotional and spiritual well-being. Practices such as mindfulness, meditation, and reflective journaling can help students develop greater self-awareness, emotional regulation, and resilience. By incorporating these practices into educational settings, we can create a more supportive and nurturing environment that promotes holistic growth.

Another important aspect of bridging the gap between education and spirituality is the cultivation of values and ethical understanding. Education is not just about acquiring knowledge and skills; it is also about developing a sense of responsibility, integrity, and compassion. Spiritual teachings often emphasize the importance of ethical behavior and the interconnectedness of all life. By integrating these principles into the curriculum, we can help students develop a strong moral compass and a sense of purpose that guides their actions and decisions.

The concept of service and community engagement is another area where education and spirituality intersect. Many spiritual traditions emphasize the importance of serving others and contributing to the greater good. By incorporating service-learning projects and community involvement into educational programs, we can foster a sense of empathy, compassion, and social responsibility. These experiences not only enhance students' personal growth but also contribute to the well-being of the community.

Finally, the integration of education and spirituality can enhance creativity and innovation. Spiritual practices often encourage us to think beyond conventional boundaries and explore new possibilities. By fostering a sense of wonder, curiosity, and open-mindedness, we can inspire students to think creatively and develop innovative solutions to the challenges they face. This holistic approach to education not only enhances intellectual and practical skills but also nurtures the creative and intuitive aspects of our being.

9

Chapter 9: The Power of Mindfulness in Learning

Mindfulness, the practice of being fully present and aware of the moment, has gained widespread recognition for its numerous benefits in various aspects of life. In the context of learning, mindfulness can play a transformative role in enhancing focus, reducing stress, and promoting a deeper understanding of the material. In this chapter, we explore the power of mindfulness in learning and its potential to create a more effective and fulfilling educational experience.

One of the primary benefits of mindfulness in learning is its ability to enhance focus and concentration. In today's fast-paced and distraction-filled world, maintaining attention can be a significant challenge for students. Mindfulness practices, such as mindful breathing and meditation, can help students develop the ability to stay present and focused on the task at hand. By training the mind to let go of distractions and stay engaged, mindfulness can improve the quality of learning and retention of information.

Another important aspect of mindfulness in learning is its ability to reduce stress and anxiety. The pressures of academic life can often lead to feelings of overwhelm and burnout. Mindfulness practices can help students manage these emotions by promoting a sense of calm and balance. Techniques such as mindful breathing, body scans, and visualization can help students release tension and cultivate a more relaxed state of mind. By reducing stress, mindfulness can create a more conducive environment for learning and personal growth.

Mindfulness also enhances self-awareness and emotional regulation. By paying attention to their thoughts and feelings, students can develop a greater understanding of their emotional responses and triggers. This self-awareness allows them to manage their emotions more effectively, leading to improved resilience and adaptability. Mindfulness practices can help students develop a more compassionate and non-judgmental attitude toward themselves, fostering a positive and supportive learning experience.

Moreover, mindfulness can deepen the learning experience by promoting a sense of curiosity and openness. When students approach their studies with a mindful and open mindset, they are more likely to engage deeply with the material and explore new perspectives. This curiosity-driven approach can lead to a richer and more meaningful understanding of the subject matter. Mindfulness encourages students to be present and fully engaged in the learning process, enhancing their overall comprehension and retention.

Finally, the integration of mindfulness into educational settings can create a more supportive and collaborative learning environment. By fostering a sense of presence and empathy, mindfulness practices can enhance communication and relationships among students and educators. This sense of connection and understanding can create a positive and inclusive classroom atmosphere, where students feel valued and supported in their learning journey.

10

Chapter 10: The Impact of Technology on Learning

Technology has revolutionized the way we learn, offering new and innovative tools and resources that enhance the educational experience. From online courses and virtual classrooms to educational apps and interactive simulations, technology has transformed the landscape of education. In this chapter, we explore the impact of technology on learning and its potential to bridge the gap between education, gaming, and spiritual growth.

One of the most significant benefits of technology in education is the ability to access information and resources anytime, anywhere. Online courses and digital libraries provide students with the flexibility to learn at their own pace and on their own schedule. This accessibility is particularly valuable for individuals who may have limited access to traditional educational institutions. By democratizing education, technology can help bridge the gap between different socioeconomic and geographic groups, promoting greater equity and inclusion.

Interactive simulations and virtual reality (VR) are other powerful tools that enhance the learning experience. These technologies allow students to explore complex concepts and environments in a hands-on and immersive way. For example, VR can transport students to historical events, scientific laboratories, or even outer space, providing a unique and engaging learning experience. Interactive simulations can help students visualize abstract concepts, conduct virtual experiments, and develop practical skills. By making learning more interactive and experiential, these technologies can improve comprehension and retention.

Educational apps and games are also valuable resources that leverage the principles of gamification to enhance learning. These apps offer a wide range of activities and challenges that encourage students to practice and apply their knowledge in a fun and engaging way. From language learning apps to math puzzles and coding challenges, educational games can make learning more enjoyable and effective. Additionally, many of these apps provide personalized feedback and progress tracking, helping students identify their strengths and areas for improvement.

Technology also facilitates collaboration and communication among students and educators. Online platforms and tools enable virtual classrooms, where students can participate in discussions, group projects, and interactive lessons. These platforms promote a sense of community and connection, allowing students to share ideas and support each other in their learning journey. Furthermore, technology can facilitate communication between students and educators, providing opportunities for real-time feedback and personalized instruction.

However, the integration of technology in education also presents challenges that must be addressed. Issues such as digital literacy, data privacy, and the digital divide are important considerations in the implementation of educational technology. It is essential to ensure that all students have access to the necessary devices and resources, as well as the skills to navigate and utilize these technologies effectively. Additionally, safeguarding students' data privacy and security is crucial to maintaining trust and ensuring a safe learning environment.

11

Chapter 11: Embracing Lifelong Learning

Lifelong learning is the continuous pursuit of knowledge and skills throughout one's life. In a rapidly changing world, the ability to adapt and grow is essential for personal and professional success. In this chapter, we explore the importance of embracing lifelong learning and how it can enhance our quest for knowledge, bridging education, gaming, and spiritual growth.

One of the key principles of lifelong learning is the recognition that education is not confined to formal institutions. Learning opportunities exist in every aspect of our lives, from everyday experiences and interactions to hobbies and personal interests. By adopting a mindset of curiosity and openness, we can seek out and embrace these opportunities for growth. Lifelong learning encourages us to view challenges and setbacks as valuable learning experiences, fostering a sense of resilience and adaptability.

The integration of gaming and technology can play a significant role in promoting lifelong learning. Educational games and online courses provide flexible and accessible ways to continue learning at any stage of life. These resources offer a wide range of subjects and skills, allowing individuals to pursue their passions and interests. Whether it's learning a new language, developing coding skills, or exploring creative arts, gaming and technology can make lifelong learning enjoyable and engaging.

Spiritual growth is also an important component of lifelong learning. As we journey through life, our understanding of ourselves and the world continues to evolve. Practices such as meditation, reflection, and mindfulness can help us cultivate a deeper connection with our inner selves and the greater universe. This ongoing process of self-discovery and spiritual growth enhances our overall well-being and enriches our quest for knowledge. By integrating spiritual practices into our daily lives, we can maintain a sense of balance and harmony as we navigate the complexities of the modern world.

Lifelong learning also involves staying informed and engaged with the broader community. By participating in workshops, seminars, and community events, we can expand our knowledge and build meaningful connections with others. Engaging with diverse perspectives and ideas fosters a sense of empathy and understanding, contributing to our personal and collective growth. Additionally, mentoring and teaching others can be a valuable way to reinforce our own learning and share our knowledge with the next generation.

Finally, embracing lifelong learning requires a commitment to continuous improvement and self-reflection. By regularly assessing our goals, progress, and areas for growth, we can stay motivated and focused on our learning journey. Setting achievable and meaningful goals can help us stay on track and measure our progress. Additionally, seeking feedback from others and remaining open to constructive criticism can provide valuable insights and opportunities for improvement.

12

Chapter 12: The Future of Knowledge and Growth

As we look to the future, the quest for knowledge and growth will continue to evolve in response to emerging technologies, societal changes, and individual needs. In this final chapter, we explore the potential future of education, gaming, and spiritual growth, and how we can prepare for the opportunities and challenges ahead.

One of the most exciting prospects for the future of knowledge is the continued advancement of technology. Innovations such as artificial intelligence, augmented reality, and personalized learning platforms have the potential to revolutionize the way we acquire and apply knowledge. These technologies can create more adaptive and individualized learning experiences, catering to the unique needs and preferences of each learner. As we embrace these advancements, it is essential to consider the ethical implications and ensure that technology is used responsibly and inclusively.

The future of gaming also holds great promise for education and personal development. As games become more sophisticated and immersive, they will offer new opportunities for experiential learning and skill development. Virtual and augmented reality can create realistic simulations and environments that allow learners to explore complex concepts and scenarios. Additionally, the integration of gamification principles into various aspects of life can enhance motivation and engagement, promoting a culture of continuous learning and growth.

Spiritual growth will remain an integral part of our quest for knowledge, offering a deeper and more intuitive understanding of ourselves and the world. As we navigate the complexities and uncertainties of the modern world, spiritual practices can provide a sense of grounding and purpose. The future may see a greater emphasis on integrating spiritual and mindfulness practices into education, creating a more holistic and balanced approach to learning.

As we prepare for the future, it is important to cultivate a mindset of adaptability and resilience. The rapid pace of change requires us to remain flexible and open to new possibilities. By embracing lifelong learning and staying curious and engaged, we can navigate the challenges and opportunities that lie ahead. Additionally, fostering a sense of community and collaboration will be essential for addressing the complex and interconnected issues of the future.

Ultimately, the quest for knowledge is a lifelong journey that transcends traditional boundaries and definitions. By bridging education, gaming, and spiritual growth, we can create a more integrated and holistic approach to learning and development. This quest is not just about acquiring information and skills; it is about seeking a deeper understanding of ourselves and the world, and striving to make a positive impact on the lives of others. As we continue on this journey, let us remain committed to the values of curiosity, compassion, and integrity, and embrace the endless possibilities that lie ahead.

13

Chapter 13: The Synergy of Creativity and Knowledge

Creativity and knowledge are often seen as distinct entities, yet they share a profound and symbiotic relationship. Creativity fuels our quest for knowledge by encouraging us to think outside the box, explore new ideas, and challenge conventional wisdom. In this chapter, we delve into the synergy of creativity and knowledge and how it can enhance our learning and personal growth.

Creativity is the ability to generate novel and valuable ideas. It involves thinking in unconventional ways, making connections between seemingly unrelated concepts, and approaching problems with a fresh perspective. By fostering creativity, we can enhance our capacity for innovation and discovery. This creative approach to learning encourages us to ask questions, seek out new experiences, and explore diverse fields of knowledge. Whether through artistic expression, scientific inquiry, or entrepreneurial ventures, creativity is a driving force behind our quest for knowledge.

The integration of creativity into education can transform the learning experience. Traditional education often emphasizes rote memorization and standardized testing, which can stifle creativity and limit critical thinking. By incorporating creative activities and projects into the curriculum, we can encourage students to think more independently and develop their unique talents. This approach not only makes learning more engaging but also helps students develop important skills such as problem-solving, adaptability, and resilience.

Furthermore, creativity can enhance our understanding of complex concepts. By using creative methods such as storytelling, visual arts, and interactive simulations, we can present information in a more accessible and relatable way. These creative techniques can help students grasp abstract concepts, make connections between different subjects, and retain information more effectively. By embracing the synergy of creativity and knowledge, we can create a richer and more dynamic learning experience.

Creativity also plays a crucial role in spiritual growth. Spiritual practices often involve exploring the mysteries of existence, seeking deeper meanings, and connecting with the transcendent. This exploration requires a creative and open-minded approach, allowing us to go beyond the limitations of logic and reason. By nurturing our creativity, we can develop a deeper sense of wonder and curiosity, enhancing our spiritual journey and enriching our quest for knowledge.

14

Chapter 14: Cultivating a Growth Mindset

A growth mindset is the belief that our abilities and intelligence can be developed through effort, practice, and perseverance. This mindset contrasts with a fixed mindset, which holds that our talents and intelligence are static and unchangeable. In this chapter, we explore the importance of cultivating a growth mindset and its impact on our quest for knowledge, gaming, and spiritual growth.

A growth mindset encourages us to embrace challenges and view setbacks as opportunities for learning and growth. Rather than being discouraged by failure, we see it as a valuable part of the learning process. This perspective fosters resilience and determination, enabling us to persist in the face of obstacles and continue our pursuit of knowledge. By adopting a growth mindset, we can unlock our full potential and achieve greater success in our educational and personal endeavors.

In the context of gaming, a growth mindset can enhance our experience and performance. Games often present players with challenging tasks and puzzles that require perseverance and strategic thinking. By approaching these challenges with a growth mindset, we can develop problem-solving skills, adaptability, and patience. This mindset encourages us to experiment with different strategies, learn from our mistakes, and continuously improve our skills. As a result, gaming becomes not only a source of entertainment but also a valuable tool for personal development.

Spiritual growth also benefits from a growth mindset. The journey of self-discovery and spiritual exploration is often filled with uncertainties and challenges. By cultivating a growth mindset, we can approach these challenges with an open heart and a willingness to learn. This mindset helps us develop qualities such as humility, patience, and compassion, which are essential for spiritual growth. By embracing the idea that our spiritual understanding and practices can evolve and deepen over time, we create a more enriching and transformative spiritual journey.

To cultivate a growth mindset, it is important to focus on the process rather than the outcome. By valuing effort, practice, and perseverance, we can develop a greater sense of satisfaction and fulfillment in our pursuits. Additionally, seeking feedback and reflecting on our experiences can help us identify areas for improvement and continue our growth. By nurturing a growth mindset, we can enhance our quest for knowledge and create a more fulfilling and meaningful life.

15

Chapter 15: The Role of Mentorship and Community

Mentorship and community play a vital role in our quest for knowledge, providing guidance, support, and a sense of belonging. In this final chapter, we explore the importance of mentorship and community and how they can enrich our learning and personal growth.

Mentorship is the process of receiving guidance and support from someone with more experience or knowledge. A mentor can offer valuable insights, advice, and encouragement, helping us navigate the challenges and opportunities we encounter on our journey. Whether in education, gaming, or spiritual growth, mentorship can provide a sense of direction and purpose, enhancing our learning experience. By building a strong mentor-mentee relationship, we can gain new perspectives, develop our skills, and achieve our goals more effectively.

In the realm of education, mentors can play a crucial role in inspiring and motivating students. Teachers, professors, and coaches can serve as mentors, offering personalized guidance and support. By creating a nurturing and supportive learning environment, mentors can help students develop confidence, curiosity, and a love for learning. Additionally, peer mentorship programs can foster a sense of community and collaboration, allowing students to learn from each other and build meaningful connections.

Gaming communities also offer opportunities for mentorship and support. Online forums, social media groups, and gaming clubs provide platforms for players to share their experiences, seek advice, and collaborate on strategies. These communities foster a sense of camaraderie and belonging, encouraging players to learn from each other and grow together. By participating in gaming communities, individuals can develop their skills, build friendships, and enhance their overall gaming experience.

Spiritual growth is deeply enriched by mentorship and community. Spiritual mentors, such as religious leaders, meditation teachers, or experienced practitioners, can offer guidance and support on our spiritual journey. These mentors can help us navigate the complexities of spiritual practices, provide insights into our inner selves, and encourage us to stay committed to our path. Additionally, spiritual communities offer a sense of connection and shared purpose, allowing us to grow and evolve together. By participating in spiritual groups, retreats, and gatherings, we can deepen our understanding, share our experiences, and find inspiration in the collective wisdom of the community.

Ultimately, the quest for knowledge is not a solitary journey. By embracing the support and guidance of mentors and communities, we can enhance our learning experience and achieve greater personal growth. As we continue on this journey, let us remain open to the wisdom and insights of others, and seek to build meaningful connections that enrich our lives and the lives of those around us.

Book Description:

Embark on a transformative journey through the pages of "The Quest for Knowledge: Bridging Education, Gaming, and Spiritual Growth." This thought-provoking book explores the interconnected realms of formal education, the world of gaming, and the path of spiritual growth, weaving together a holistic approach to learning and personal development.

In this comprehensive work, you will delve into the foundations of formal education, uncovering its strengths and limitations while exploring innovative ways to enhance the learning experience. Discover how the

CHAPTER 15: THE ROLE OF MENTORSHIP AND COMMUNITY

evolution of gaming has transformed it into a powerful tool for education, offering interactive and immersive experiences that engage and inspire learners of all ages.

Explore the intersection of education and gaming, where the principles of gamification and motivation come to life, creating dynamic and engaging learning environments. Learn how to harness the power of mindfulness and spiritual practices to cultivate self-awareness, emotional intelligence, and a deeper connection with your inner self.

As you journey through the chapters, you will uncover the synergy between creativity and knowledge, the importance of cultivating a growth mindset, and the transformative role of mentorship and community. Embrace the principles of lifelong learning and prepare for the future of knowledge and growth, guided by the wisdom and insights shared within these pages.

"The Quest for Knowledge" is not just a book; it is an invitation to explore the endless possibilities of learning and personal development. Whether you are an educator, a student, a gamer, or a seeker of spiritual wisdom, this book offers valuable insights and practical strategies to enhance your quest for knowledge and create a more fulfilling and meaningful life.

www.ingramcontent.com/pod-product-compliance
Lightning Source LLC
LaVergne TN
LVHW020503080526
838202LV00057B/6130